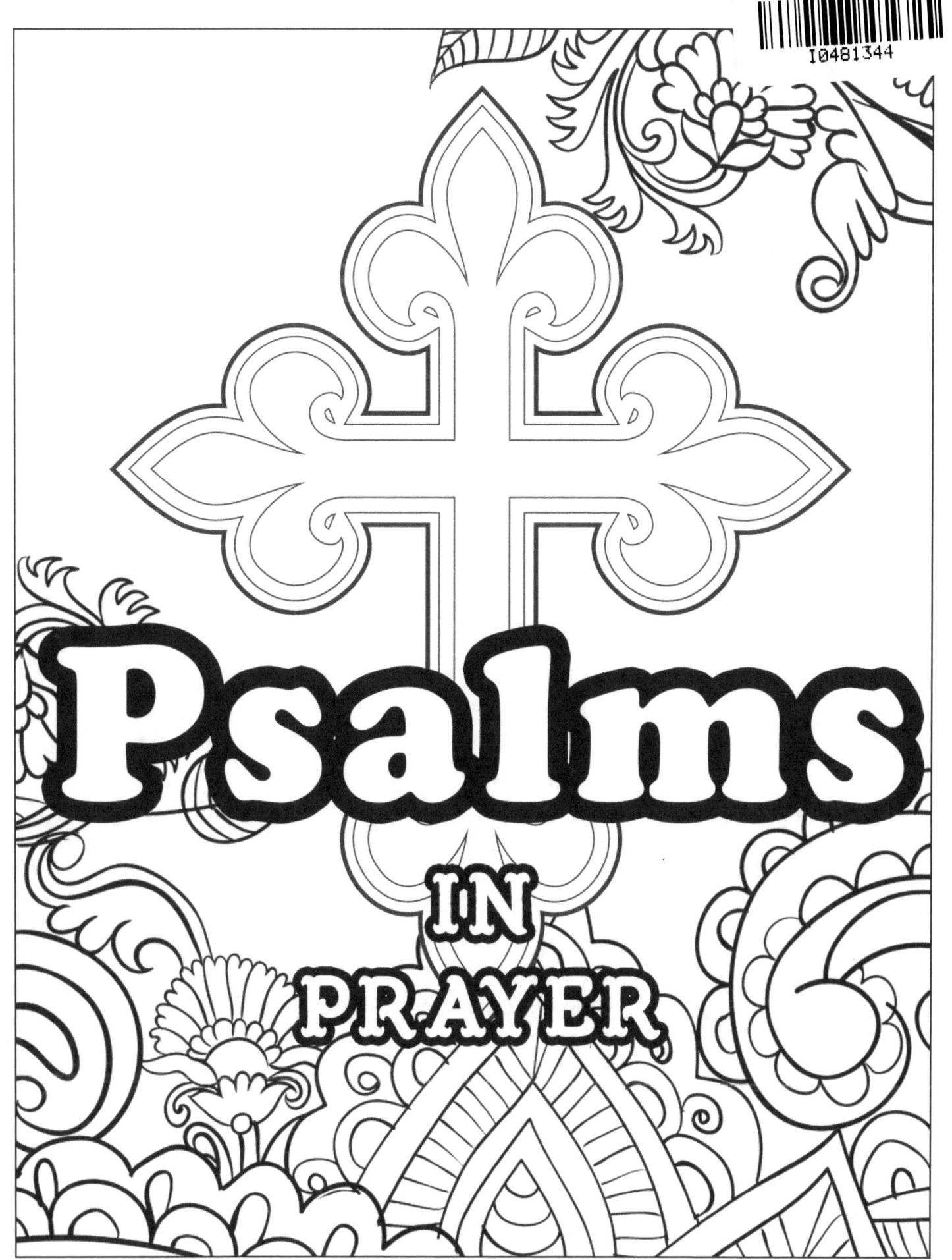

Psalms

IN
PRAYER

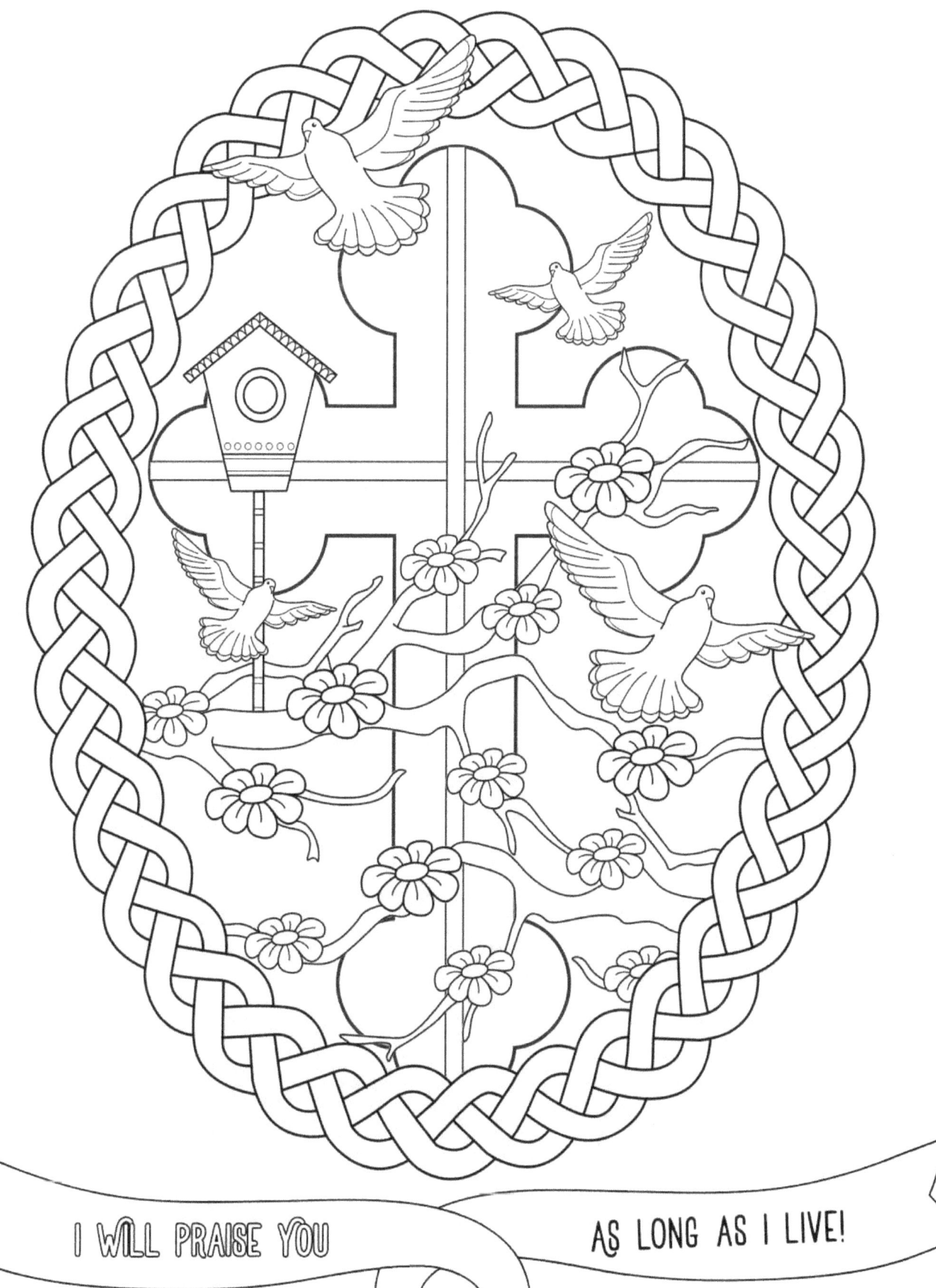

I WILL PRAISE YOU   AS LONG AS I LIVE!

IN YOUR NAME   I LIFT UP MY HANDS

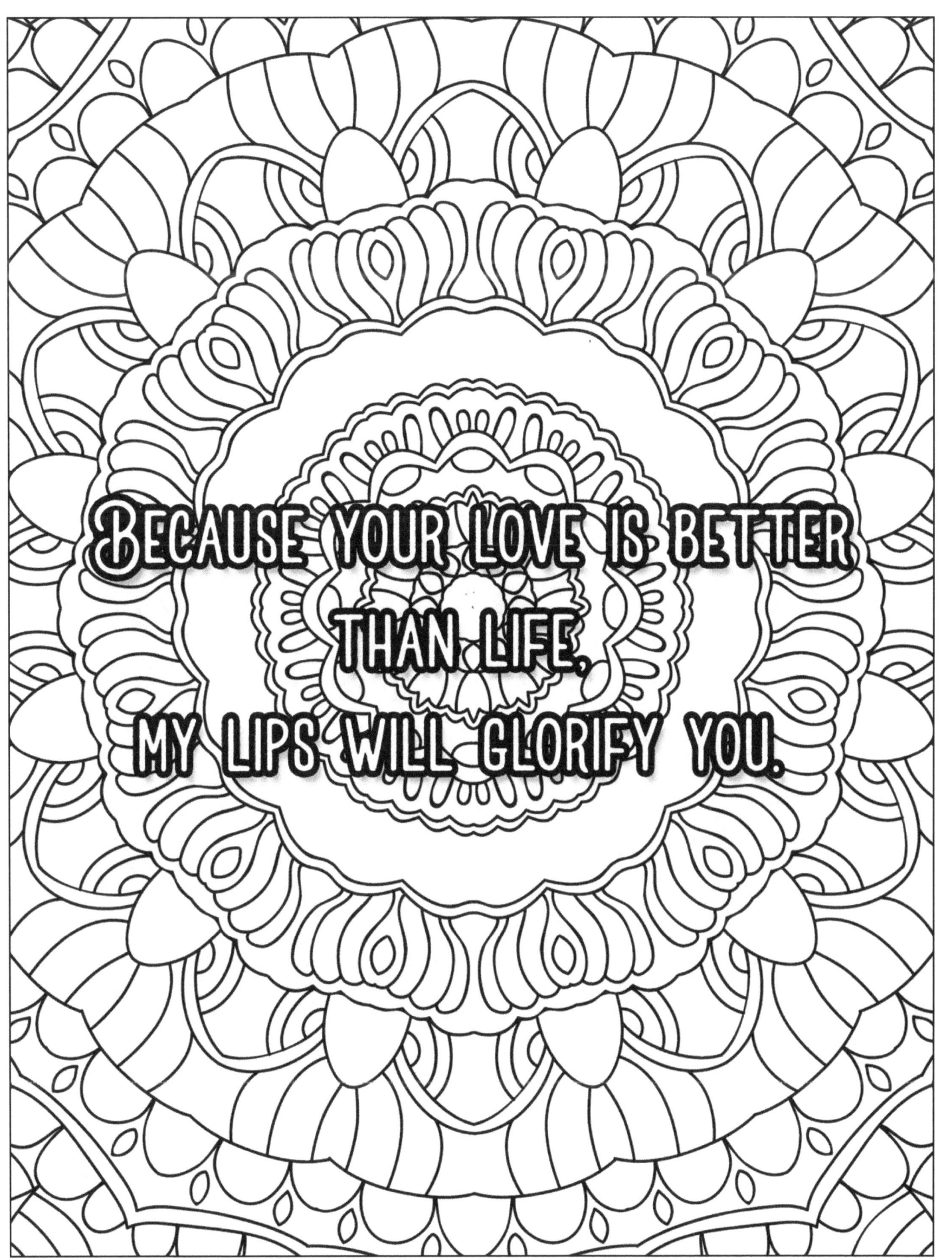

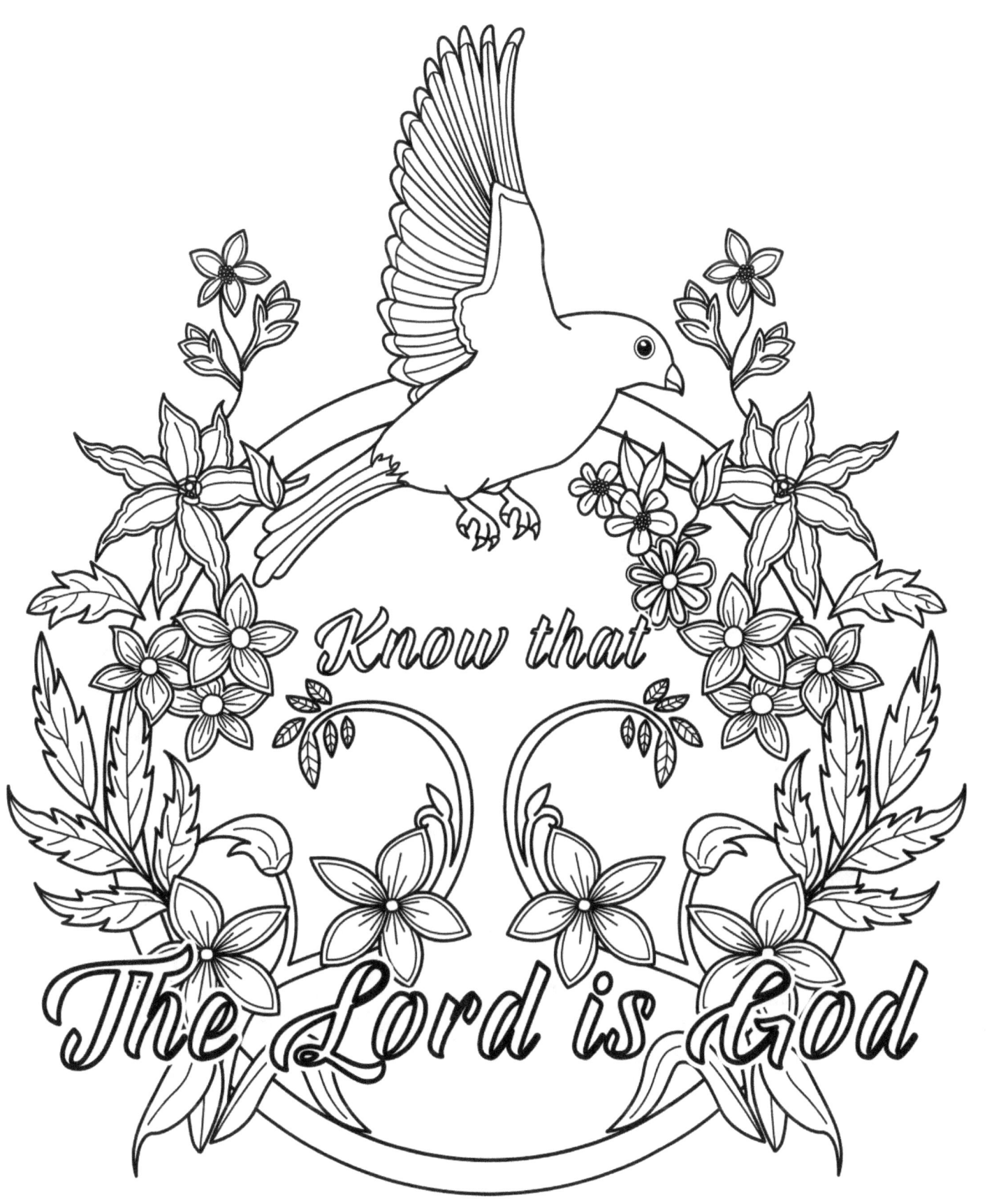

BETTER IS ONE DAY IN YOUR COURTS
THAN A THOUSAND ELSEWHERE!

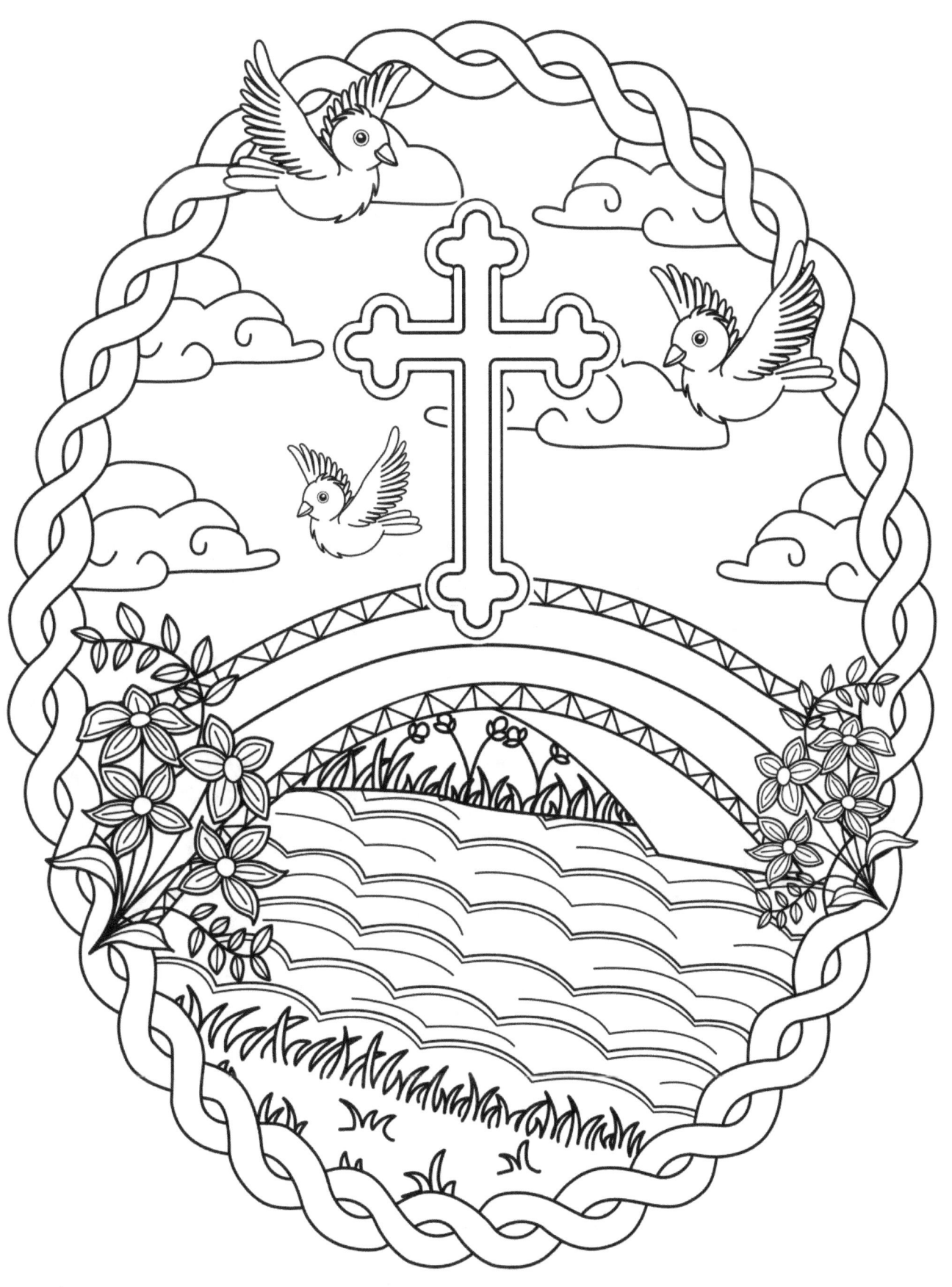

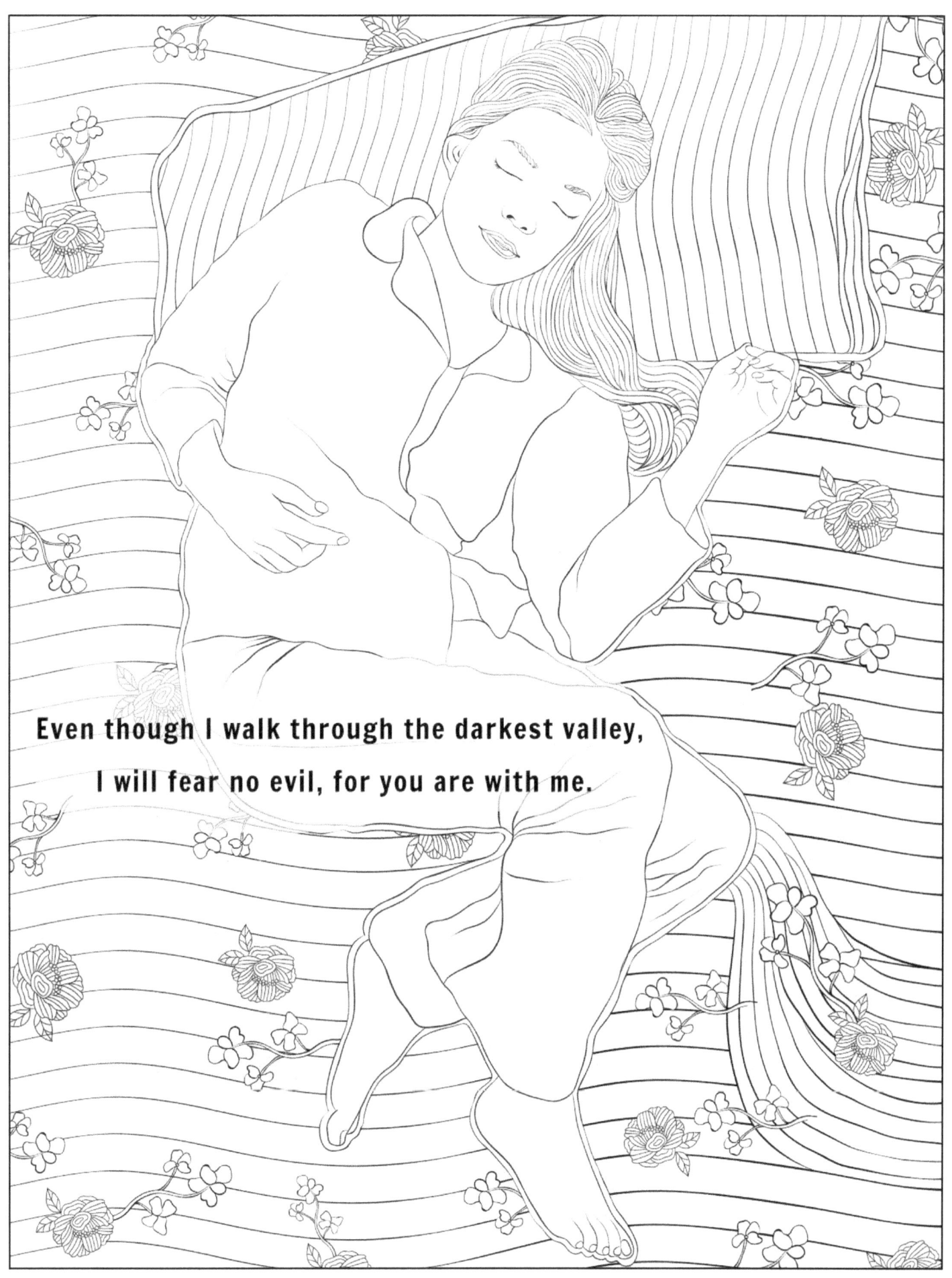

Even though I walk through the darkest valley,
I will fear no evil, for you are with me.

You anoint my head with Oil

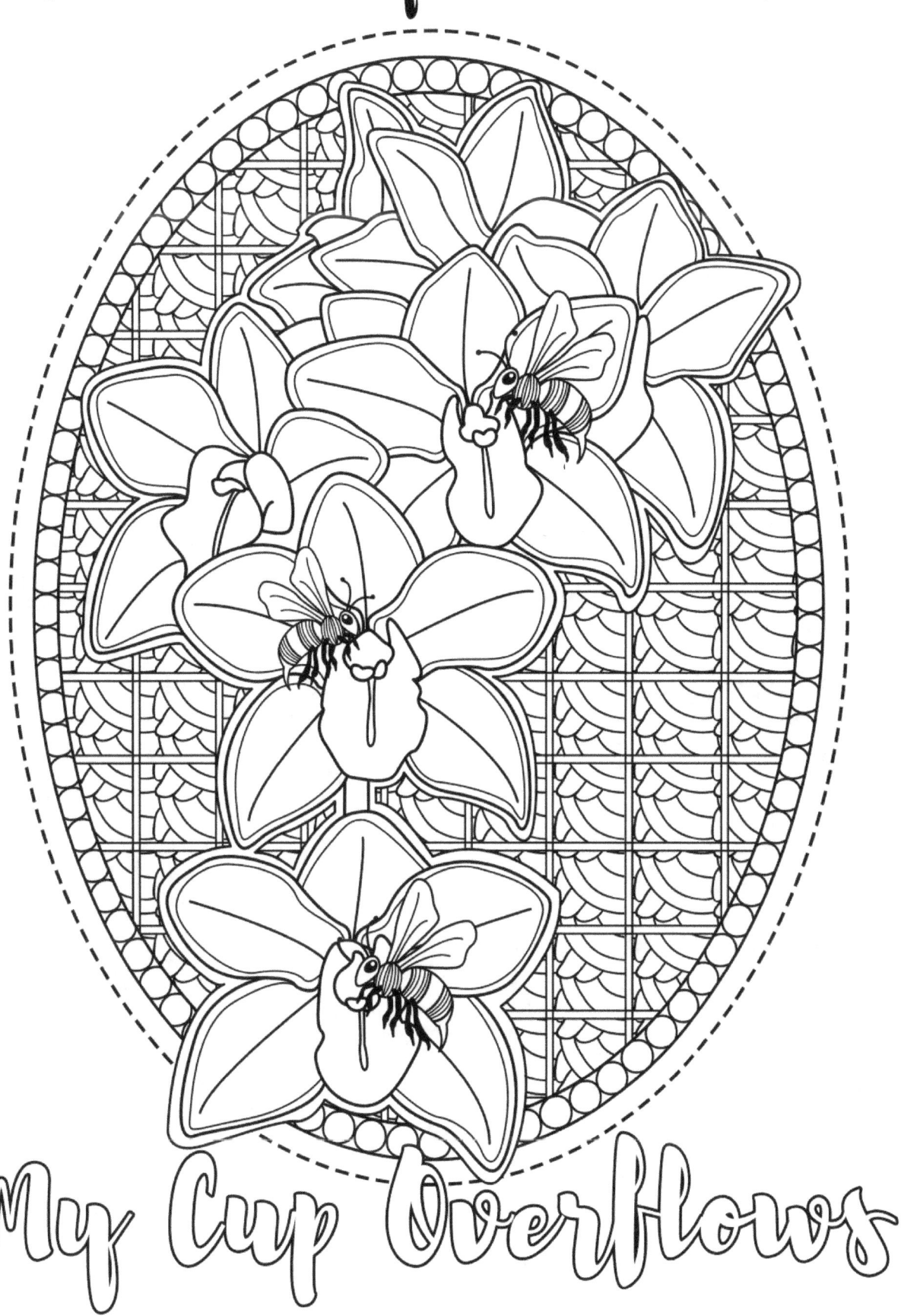

My Cup Overflows

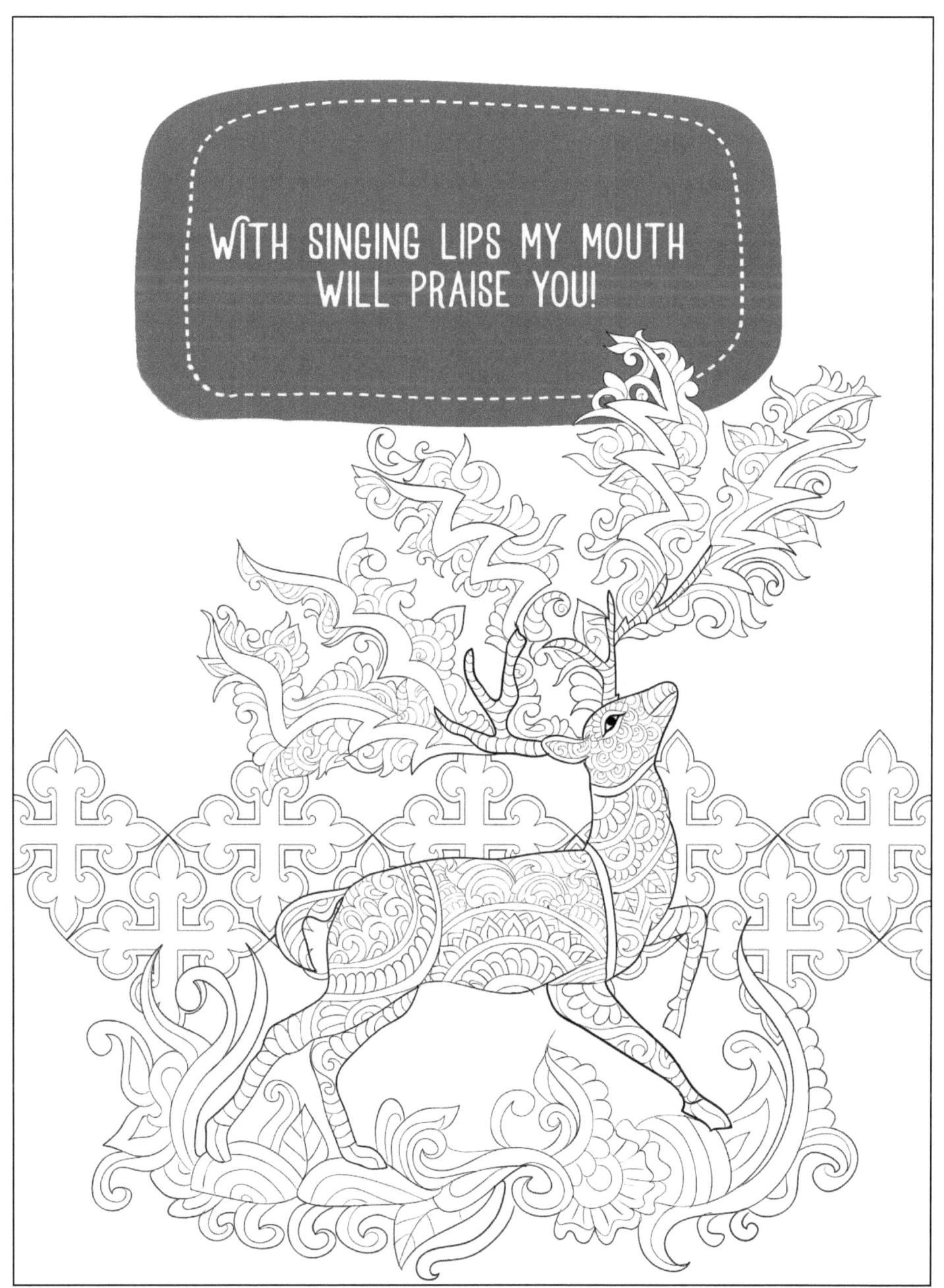

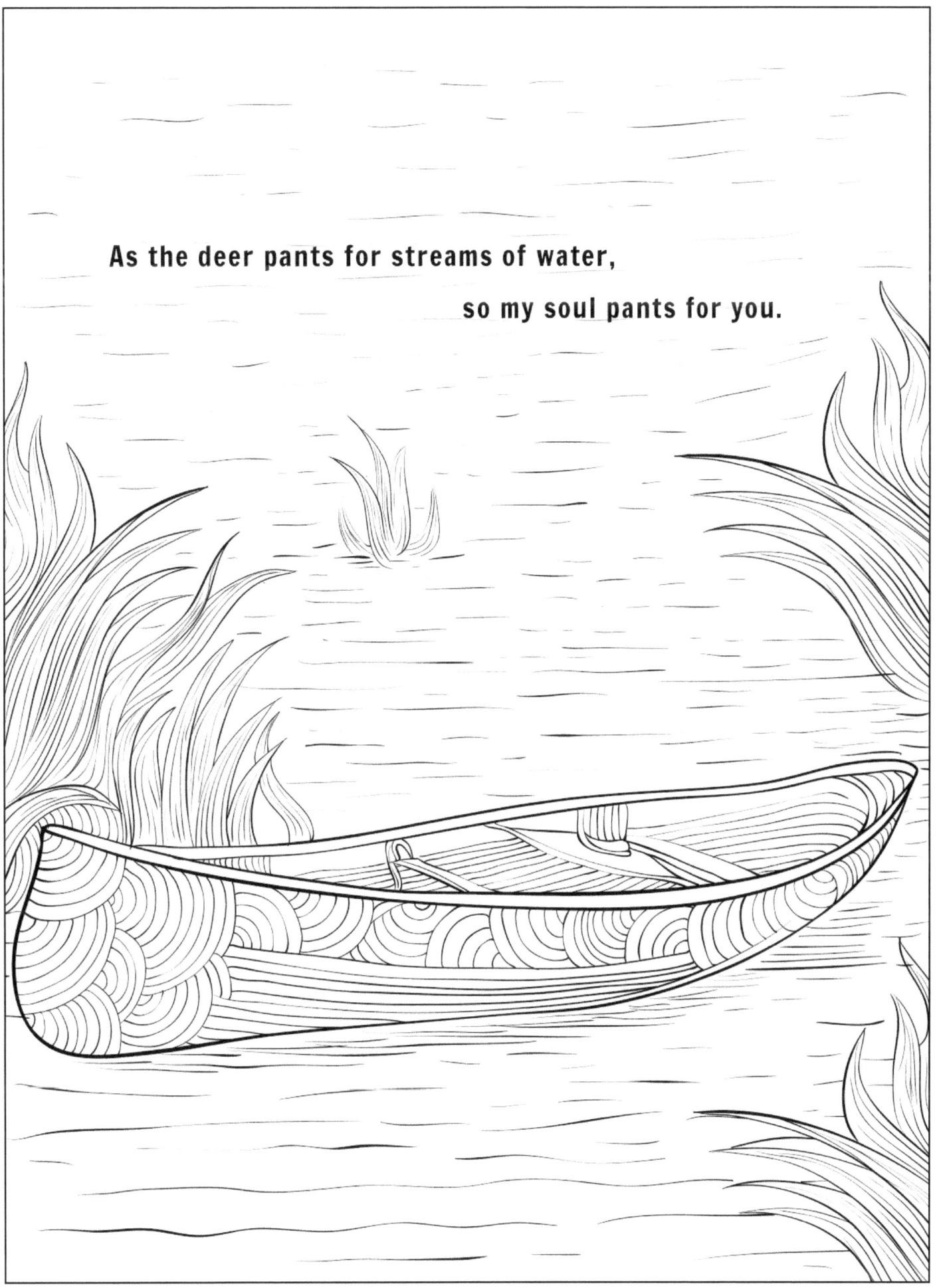

As the deer pants for streams of water,

so my soul pants for you.

SURELY YOUR
Goodness and Love
WILL FOLLOW ME ALL THE DAYS OF MY LIFE

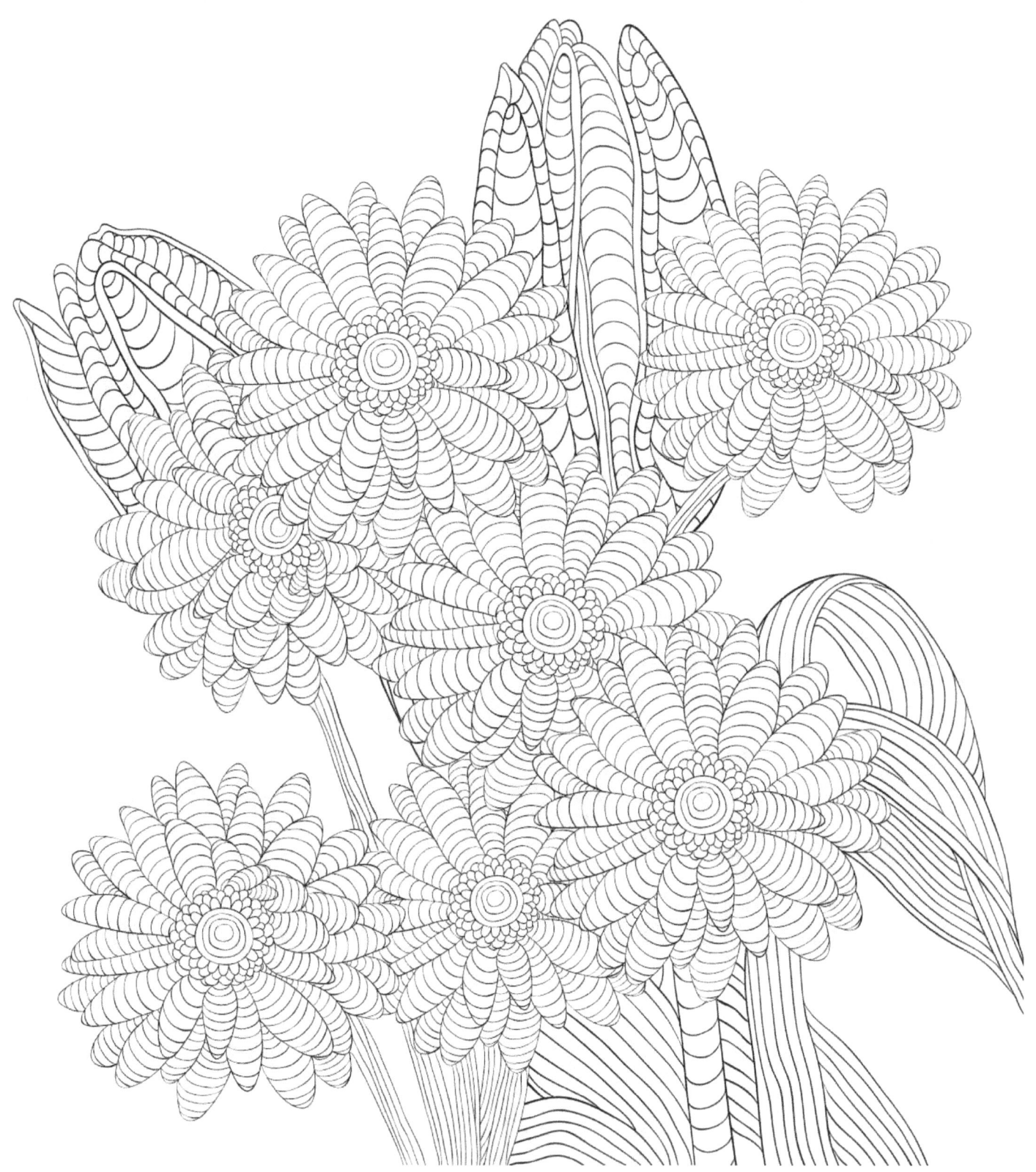

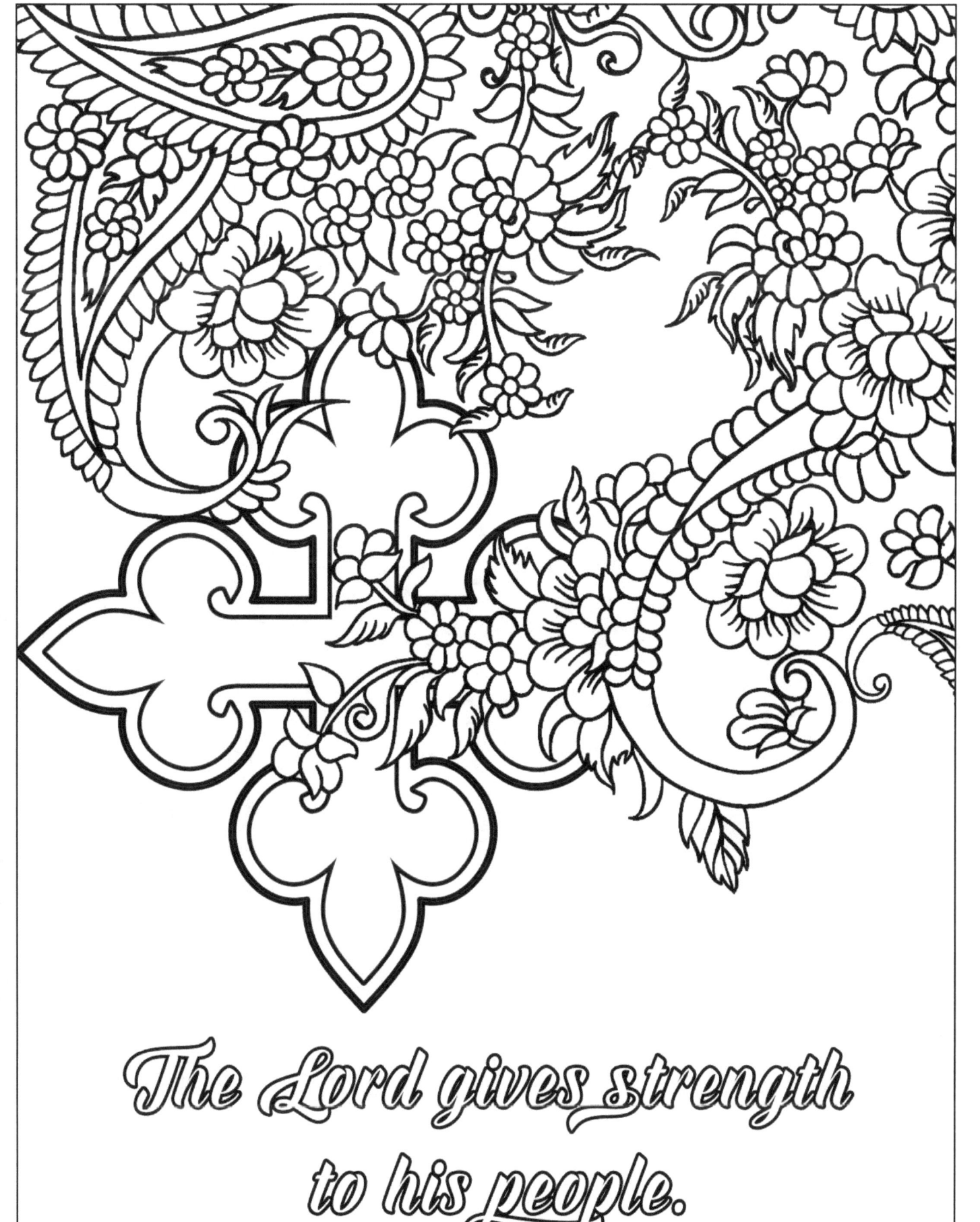

The Lord gives strength
to his people.

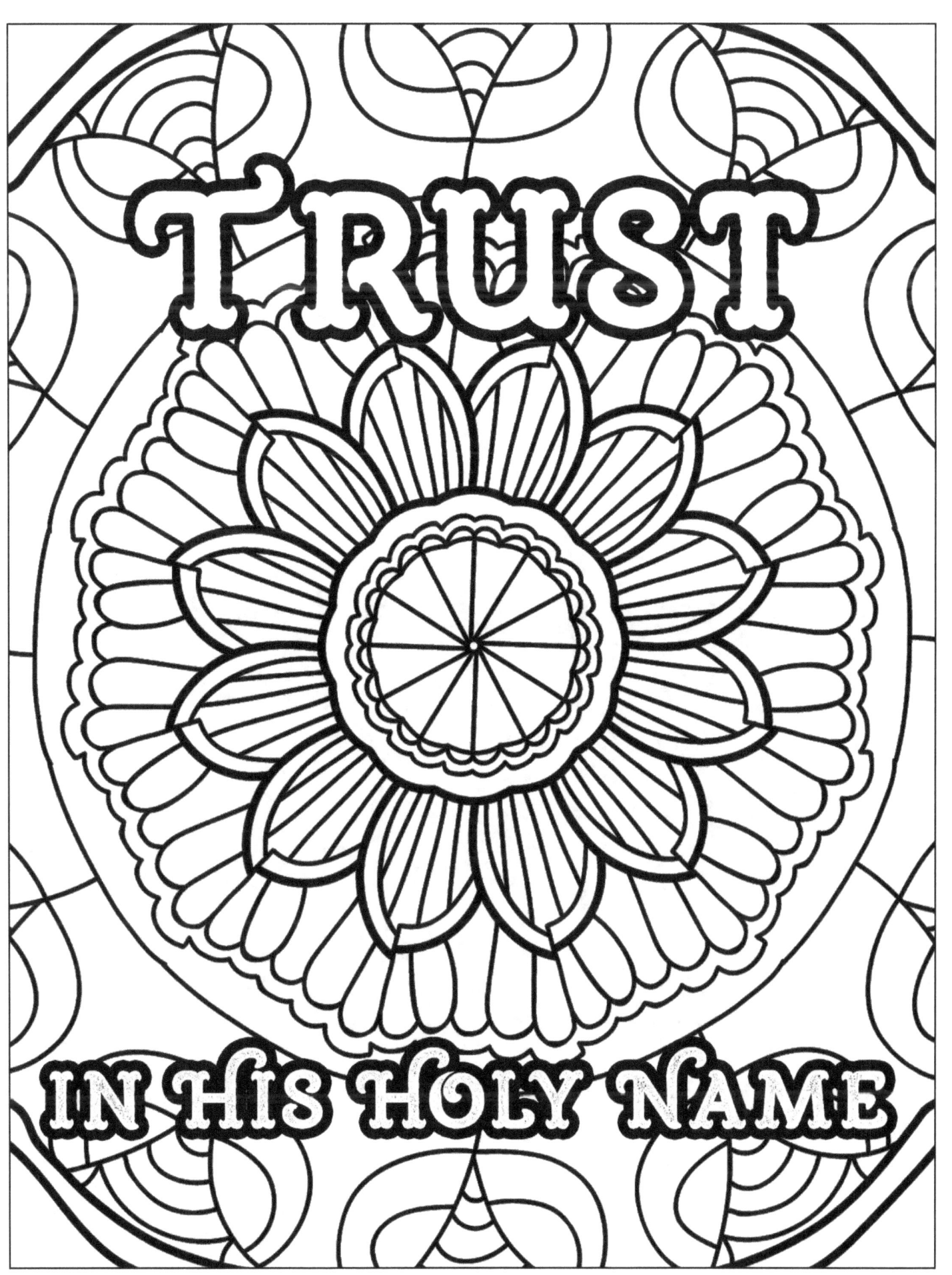

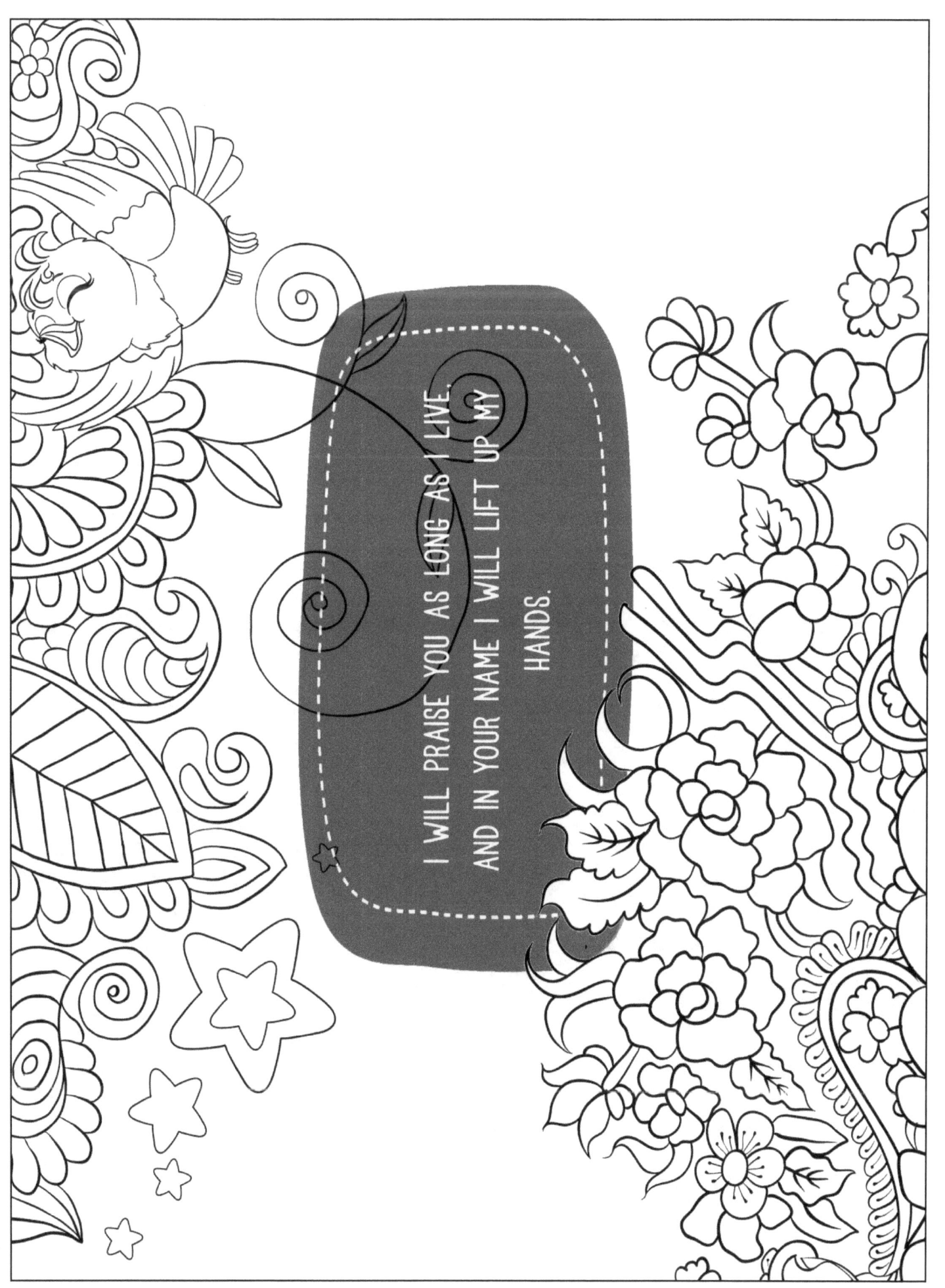

He is my refuge and my Fortress

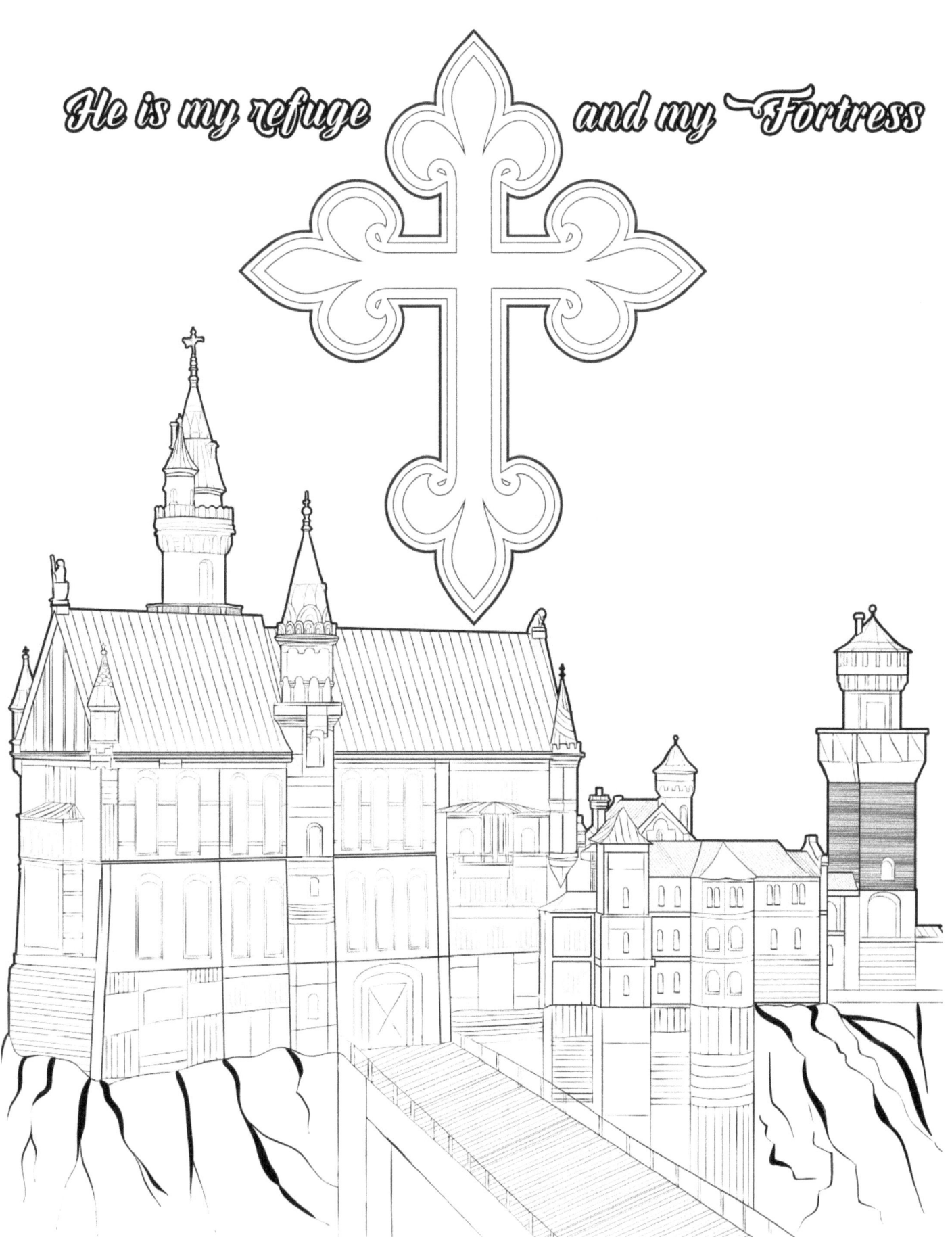

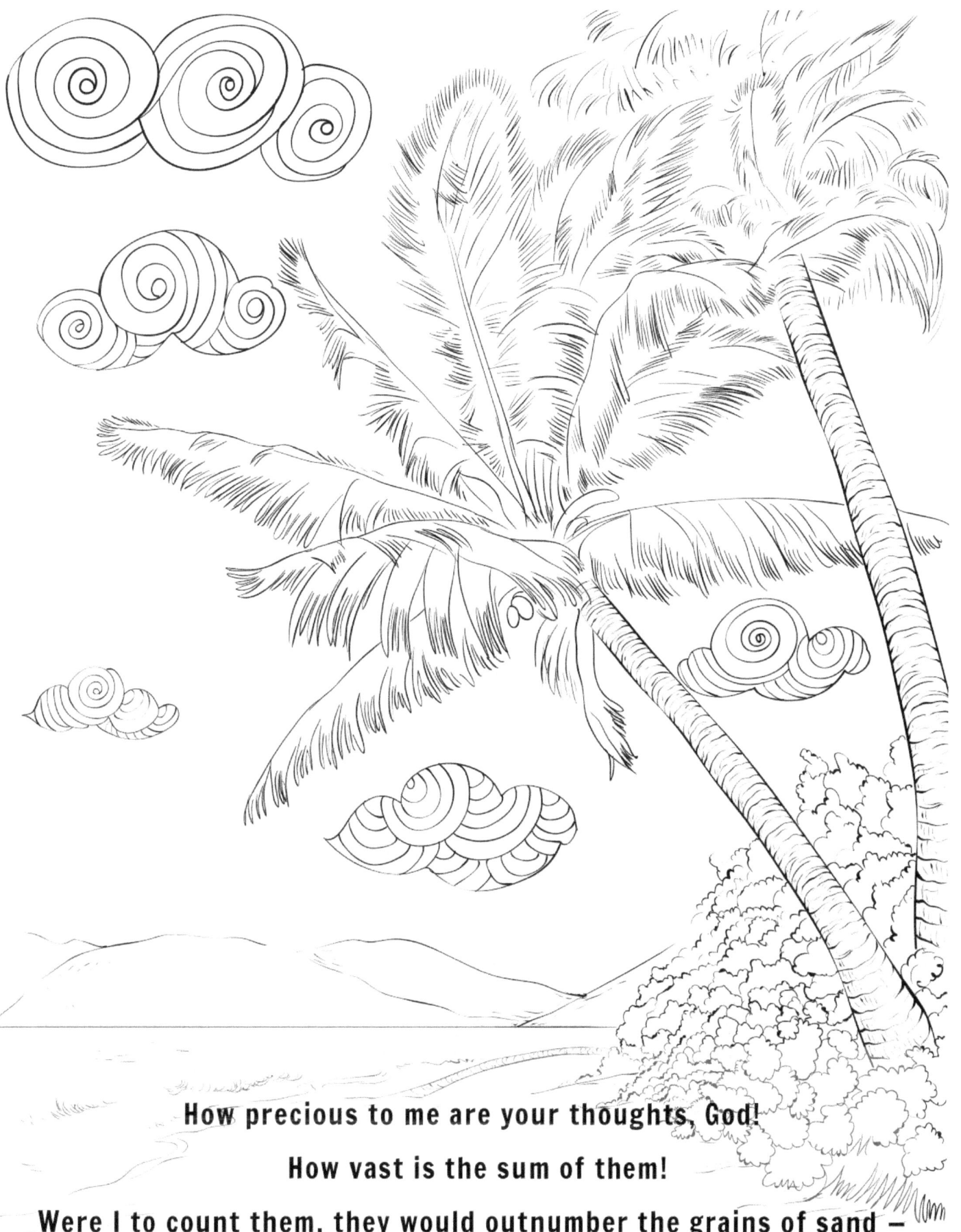

How precious to me are your thoughts, God!

How vast is the sum of them!

Were I to count them, they would outnumber the grains of sand —

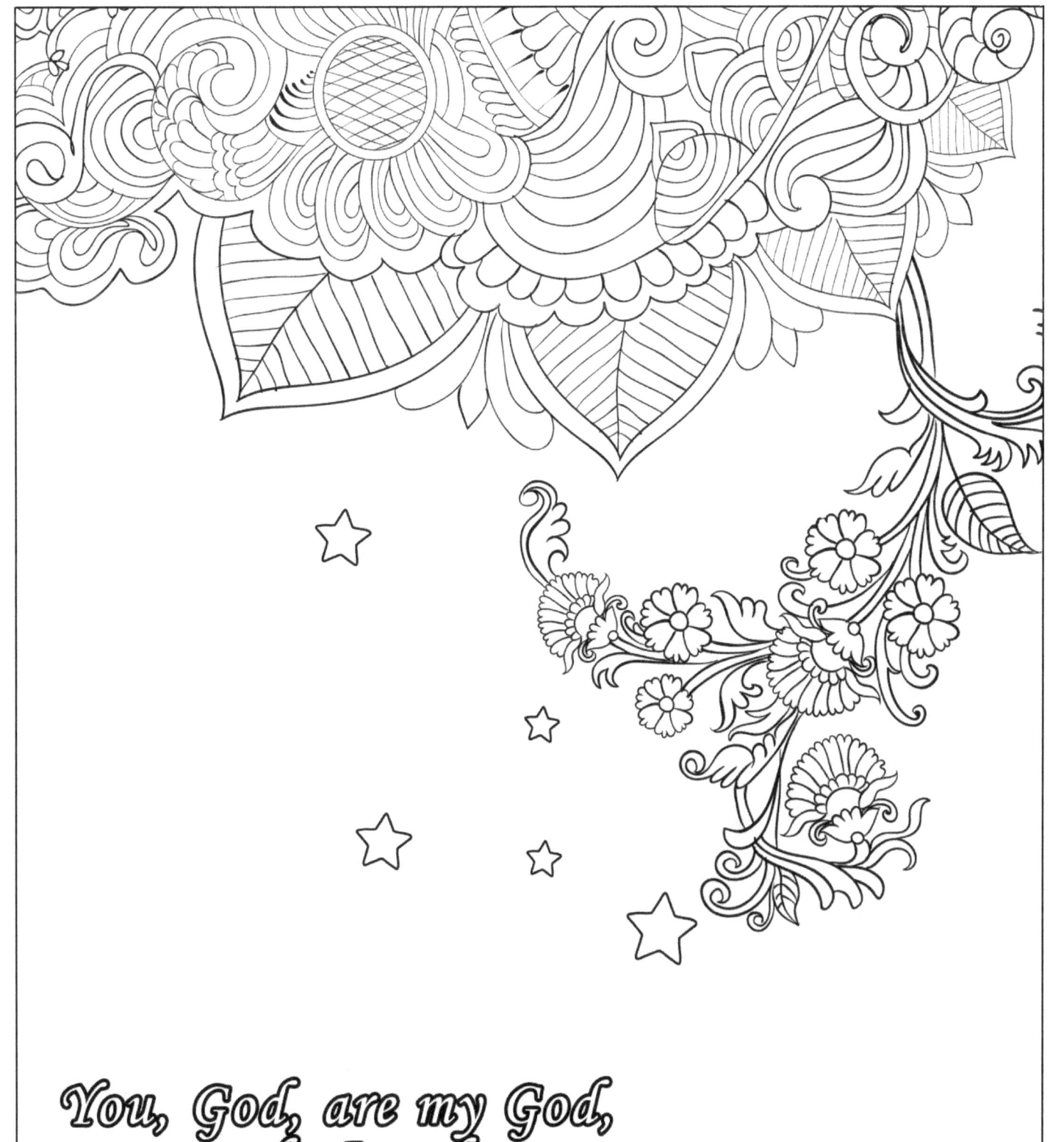

You, God, are my God,
earnestly I seek you.

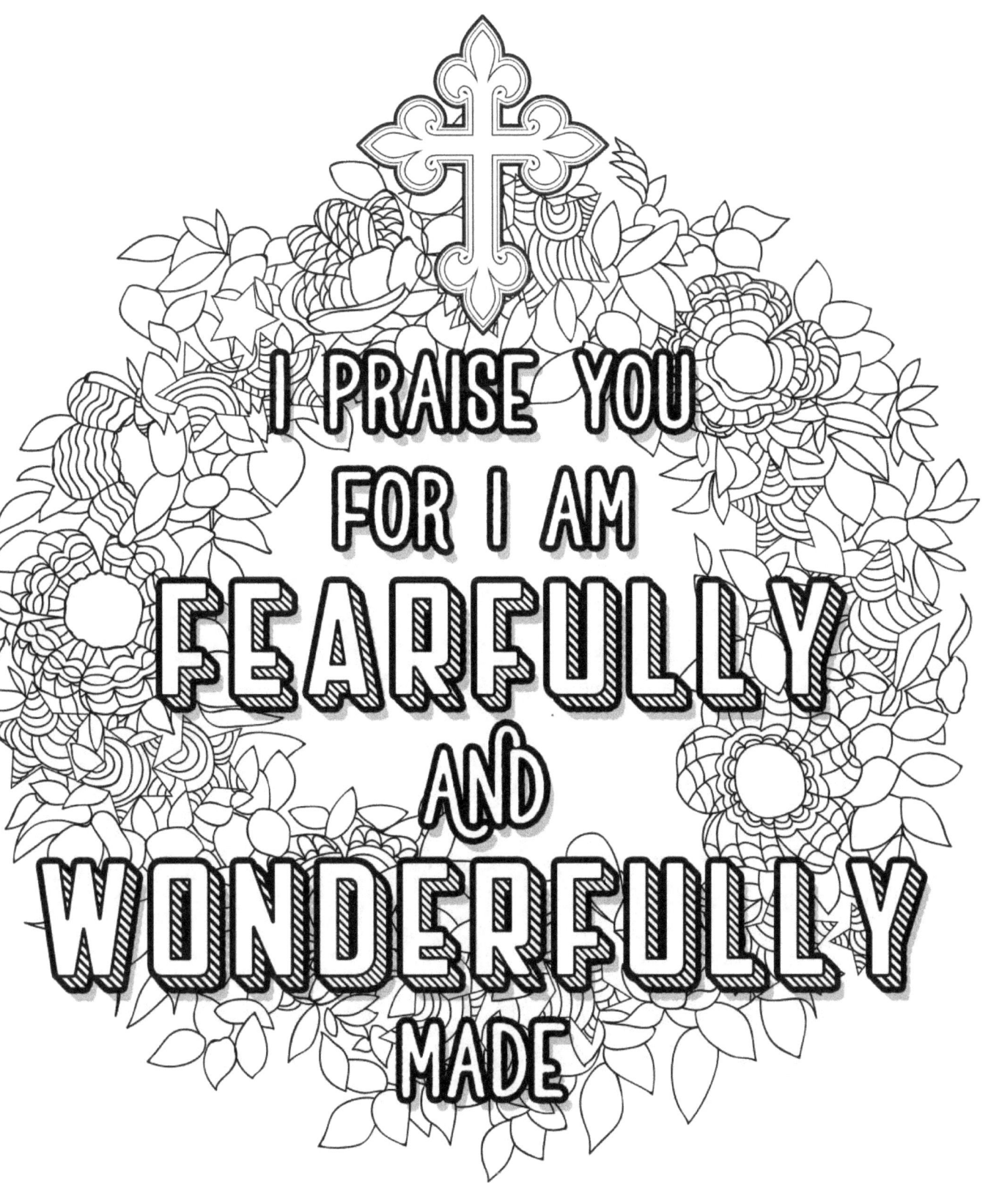

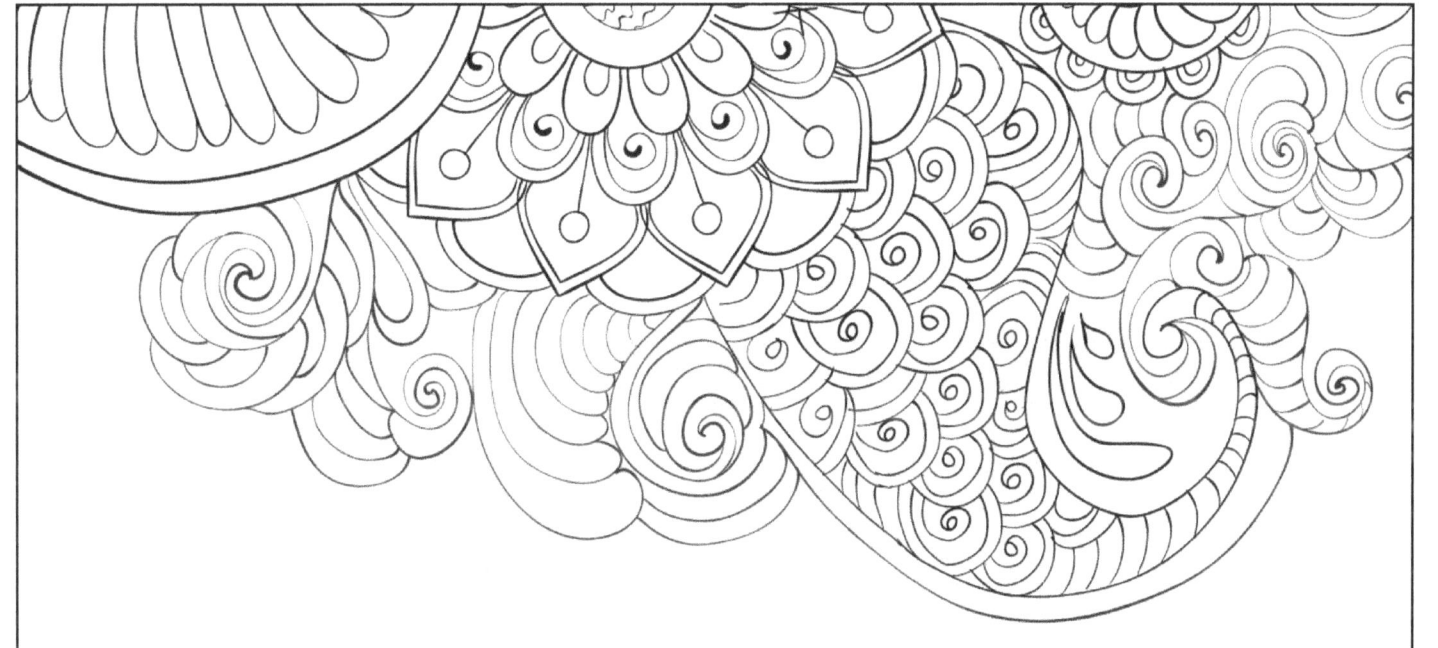

You, Lord, are a shield around me, my glory,

THE ONE WHO LIFTS
MY HEAD HIGH.

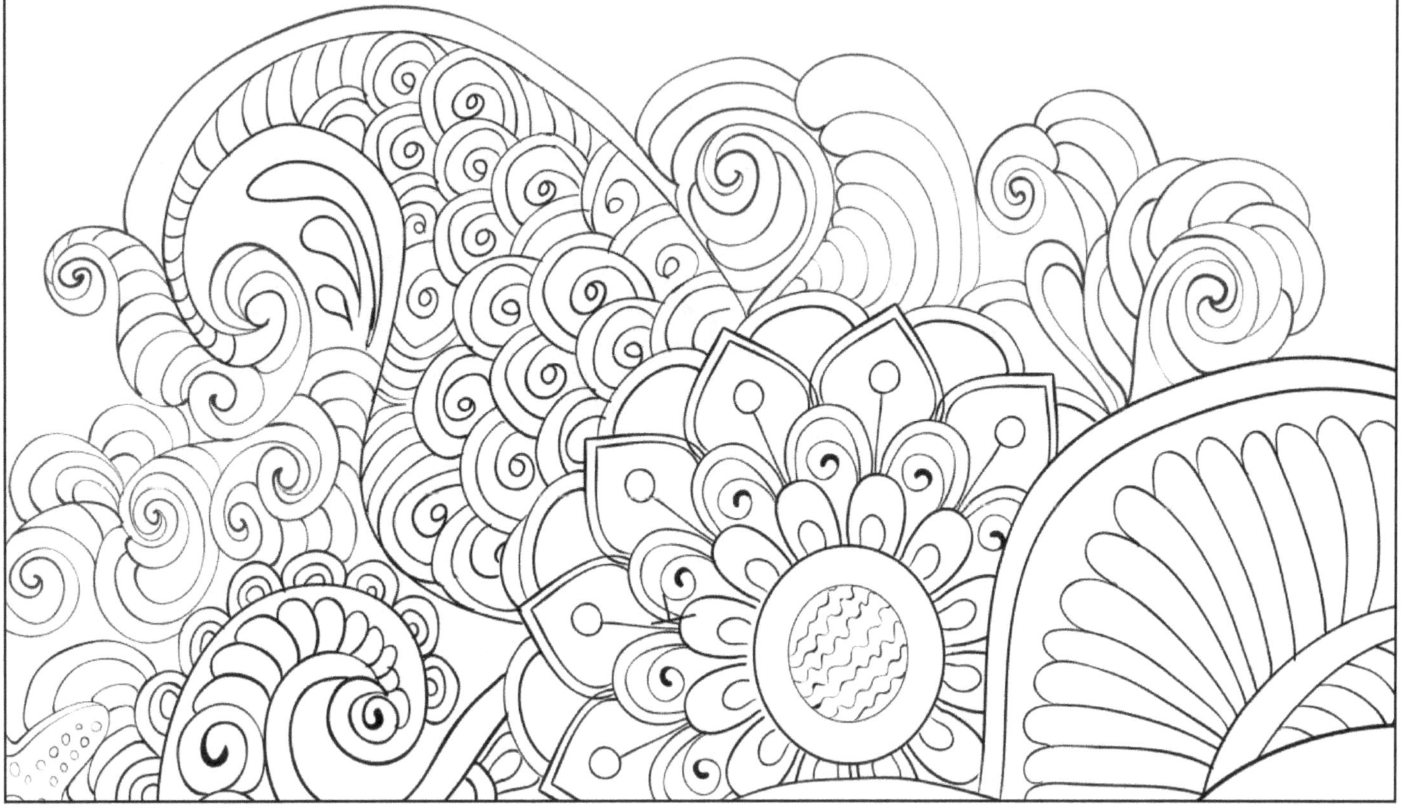

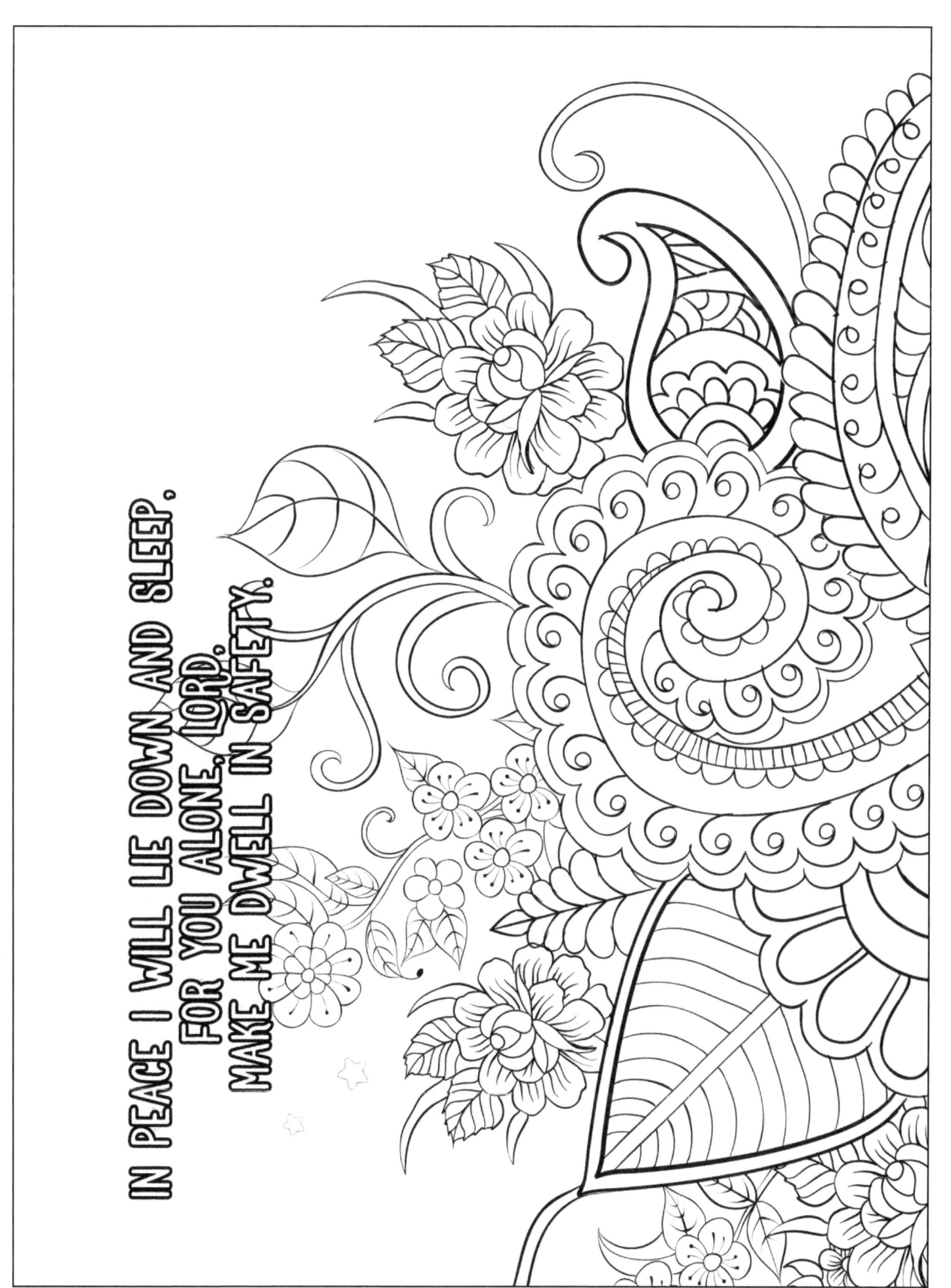

IN PEACE I WILL LIE DOWN AND SLEEP,
FOR YOU ALONE, LORD,
MAKE ME DWELL IN SAFETY.

CREATE IN ME A PURE HEART, O GOD, AND RENEW A STEADFAST SPIRIT WITHIN ME.

Restore to me the joy of your salvation and grant me a willing spirit, to sustain me.

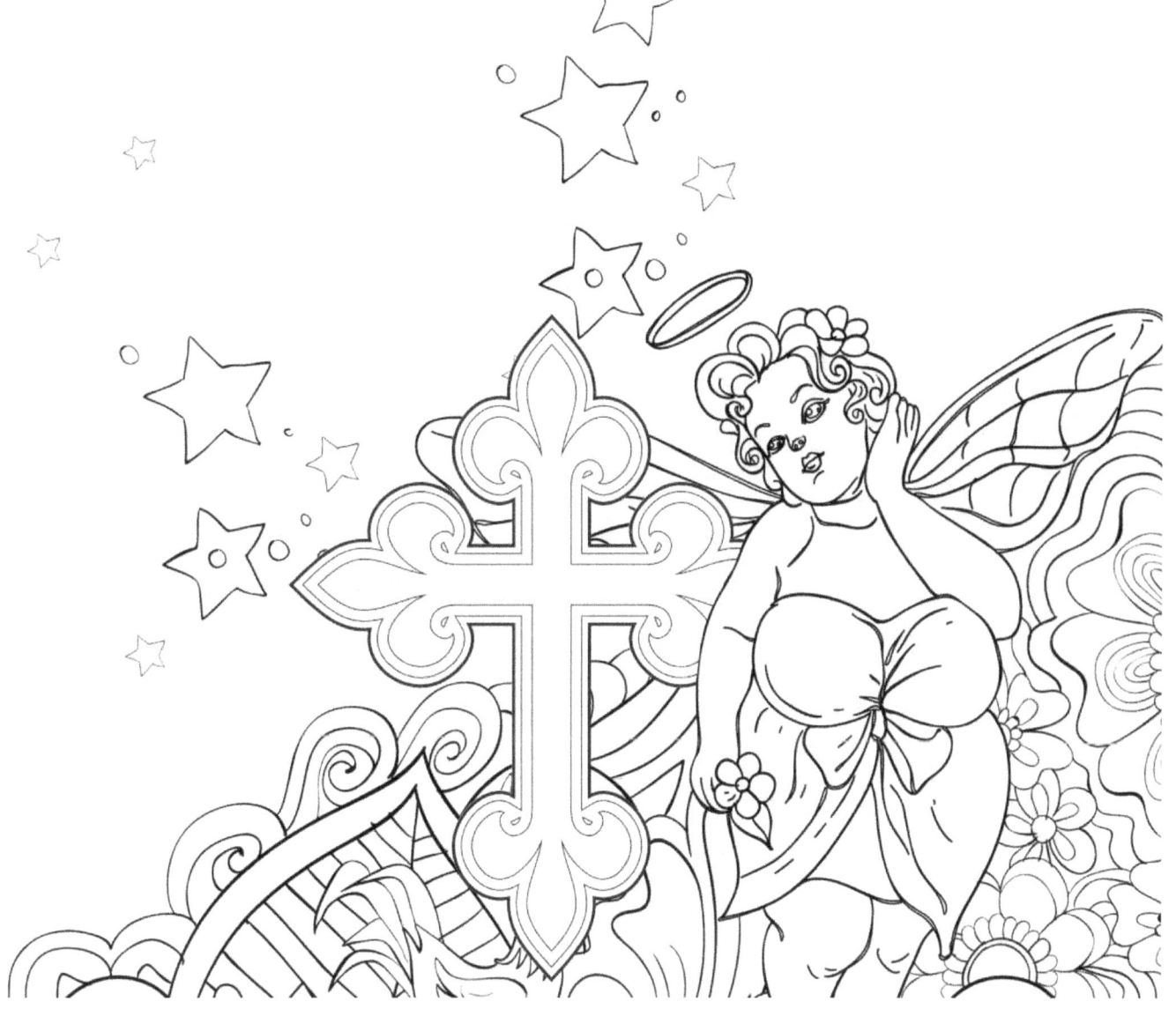

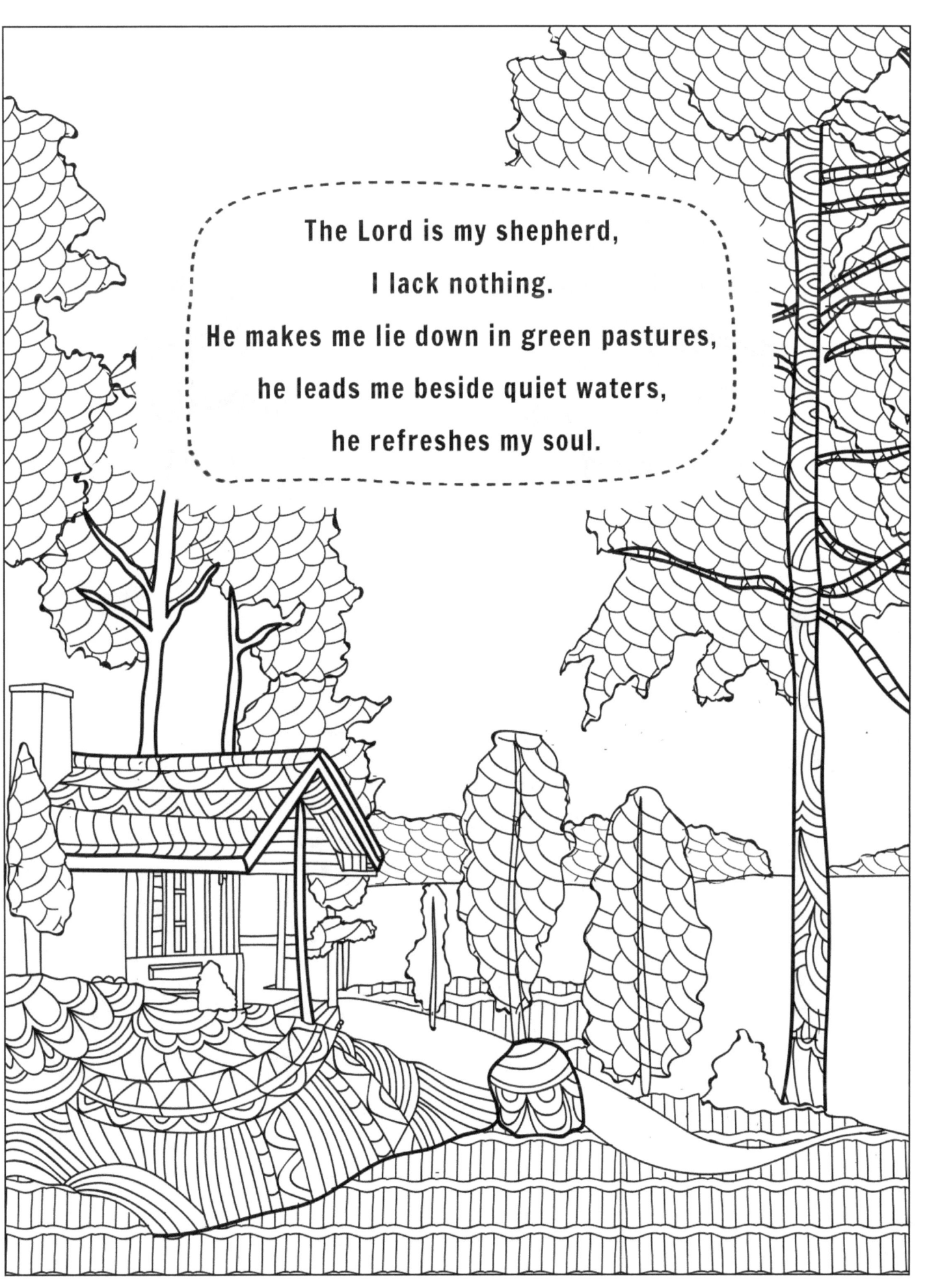

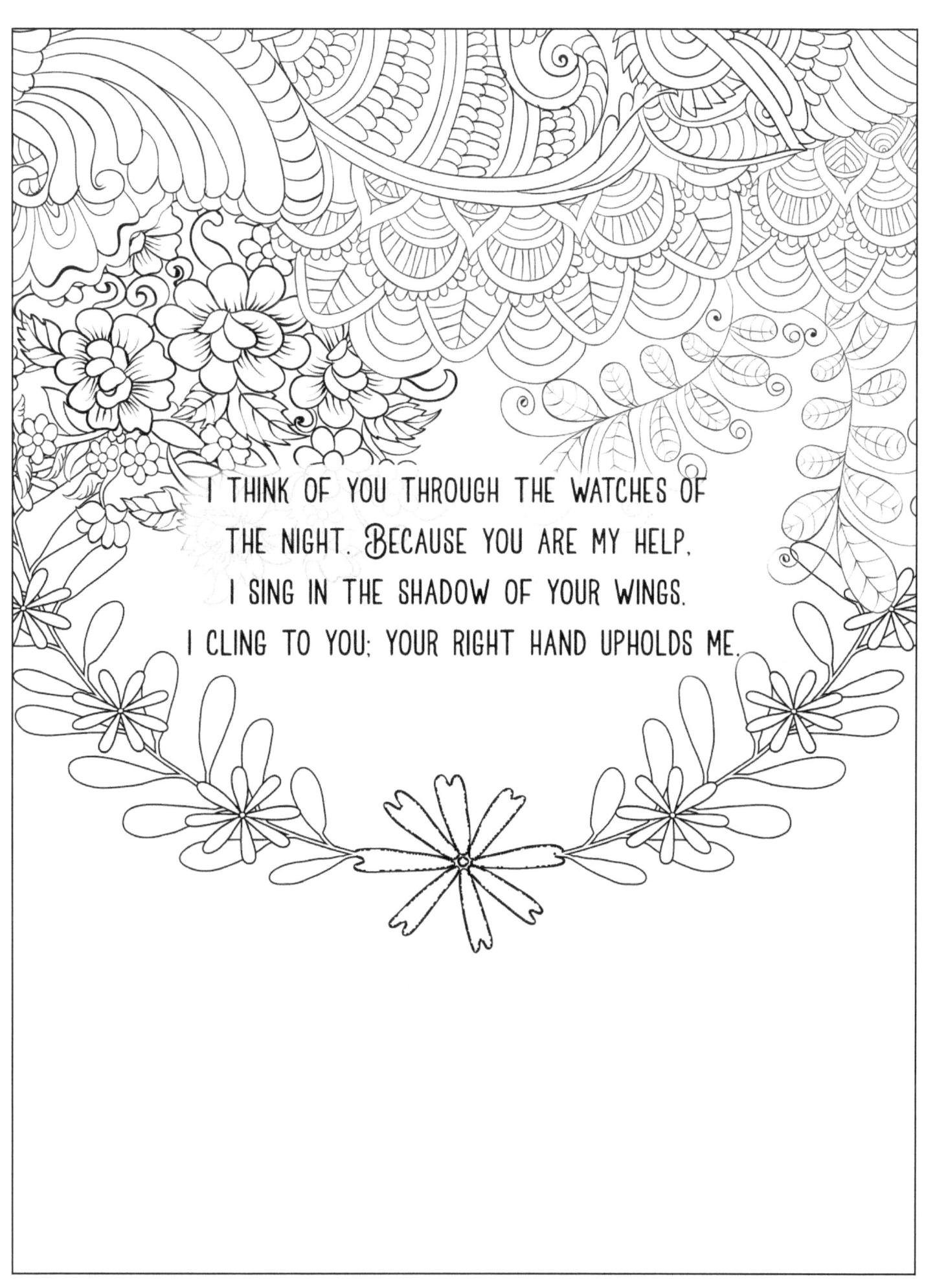

I THINK OF YOU THROUGH THE WATCHES OF
THE NIGHT. BECAUSE YOU ARE MY HELP,
I SING IN THE SHADOW OF YOUR WINGS.
I CLING TO YOU; YOUR RIGHT HAND UPHOLDS ME.

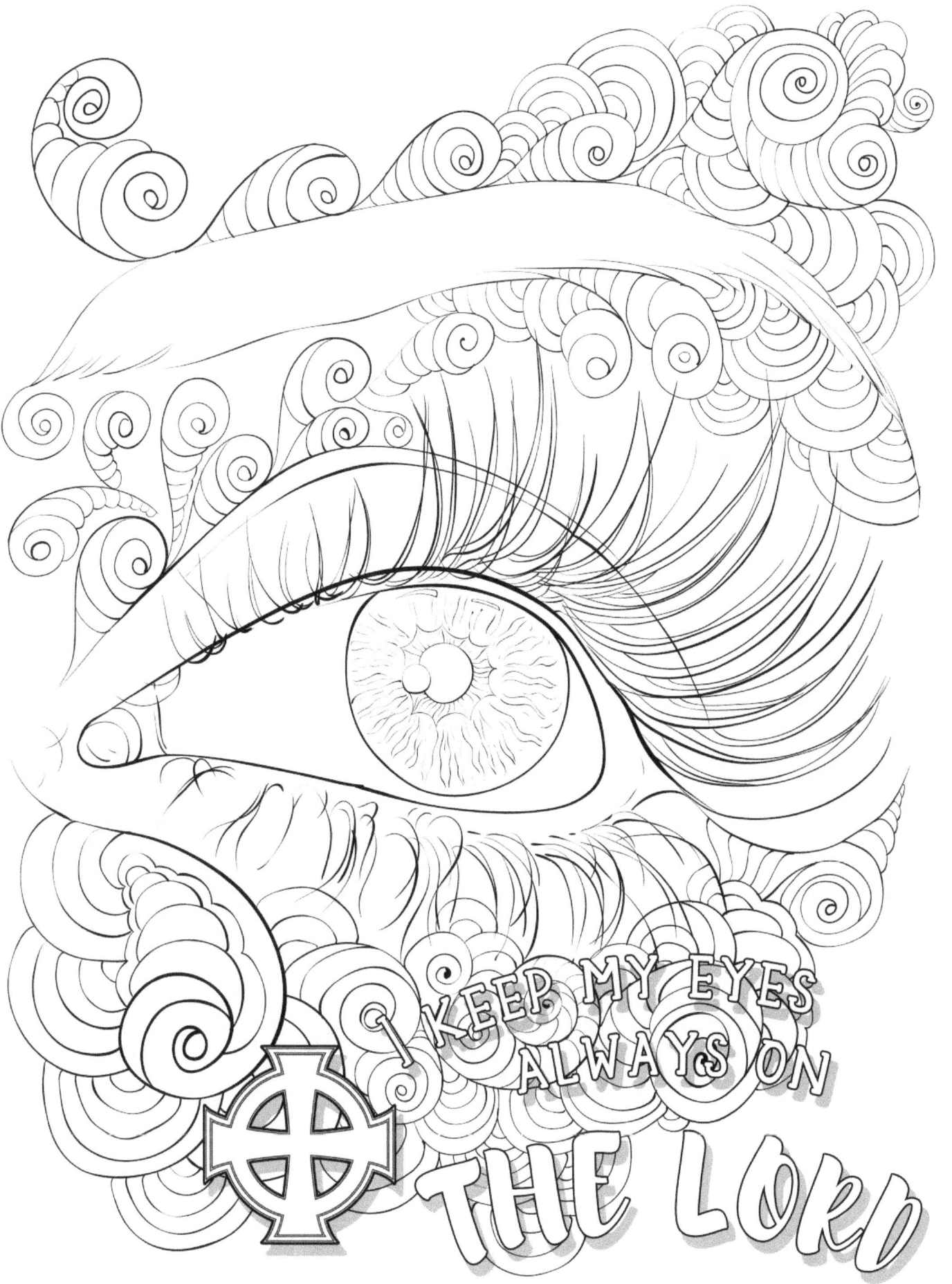

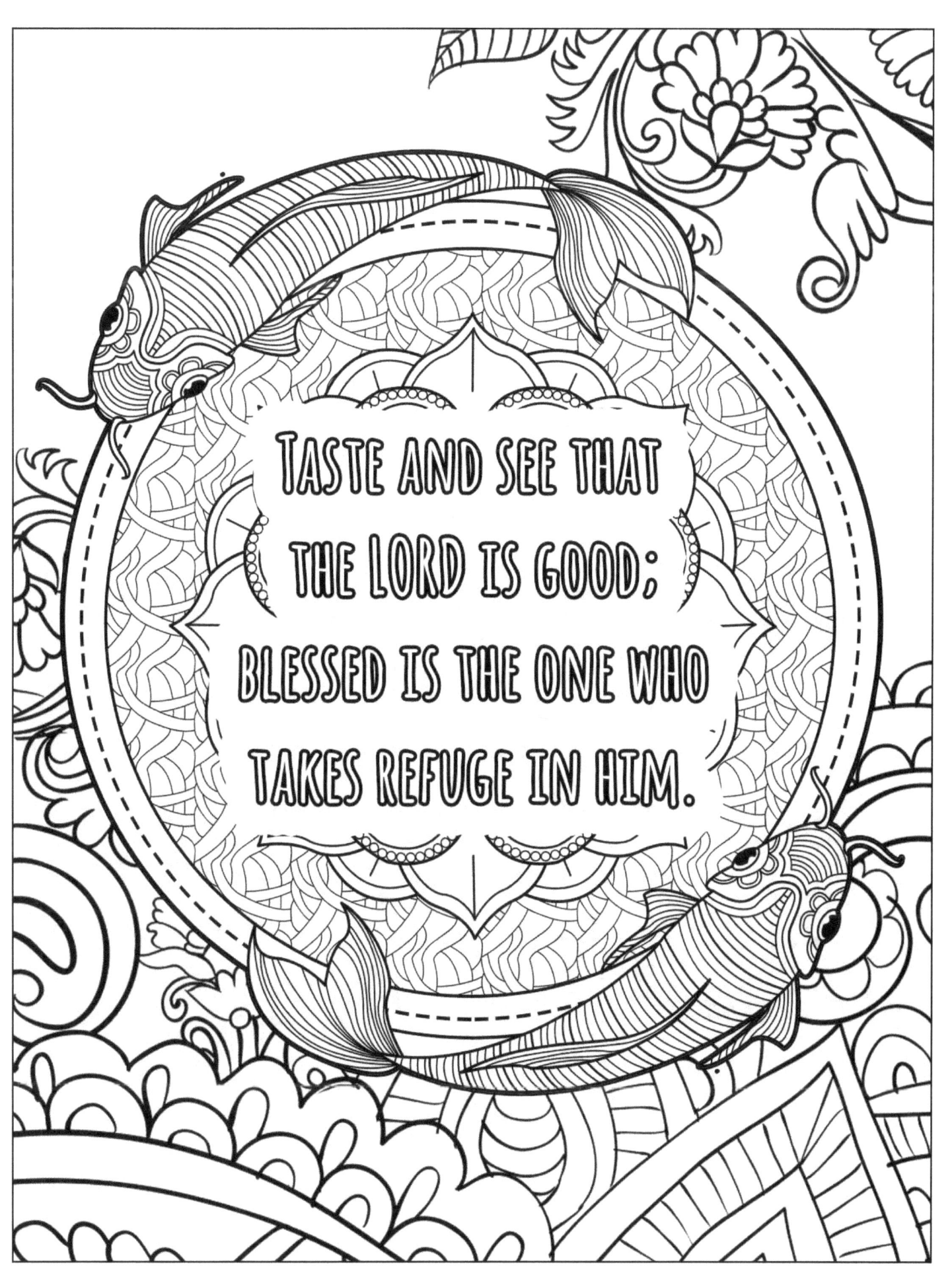

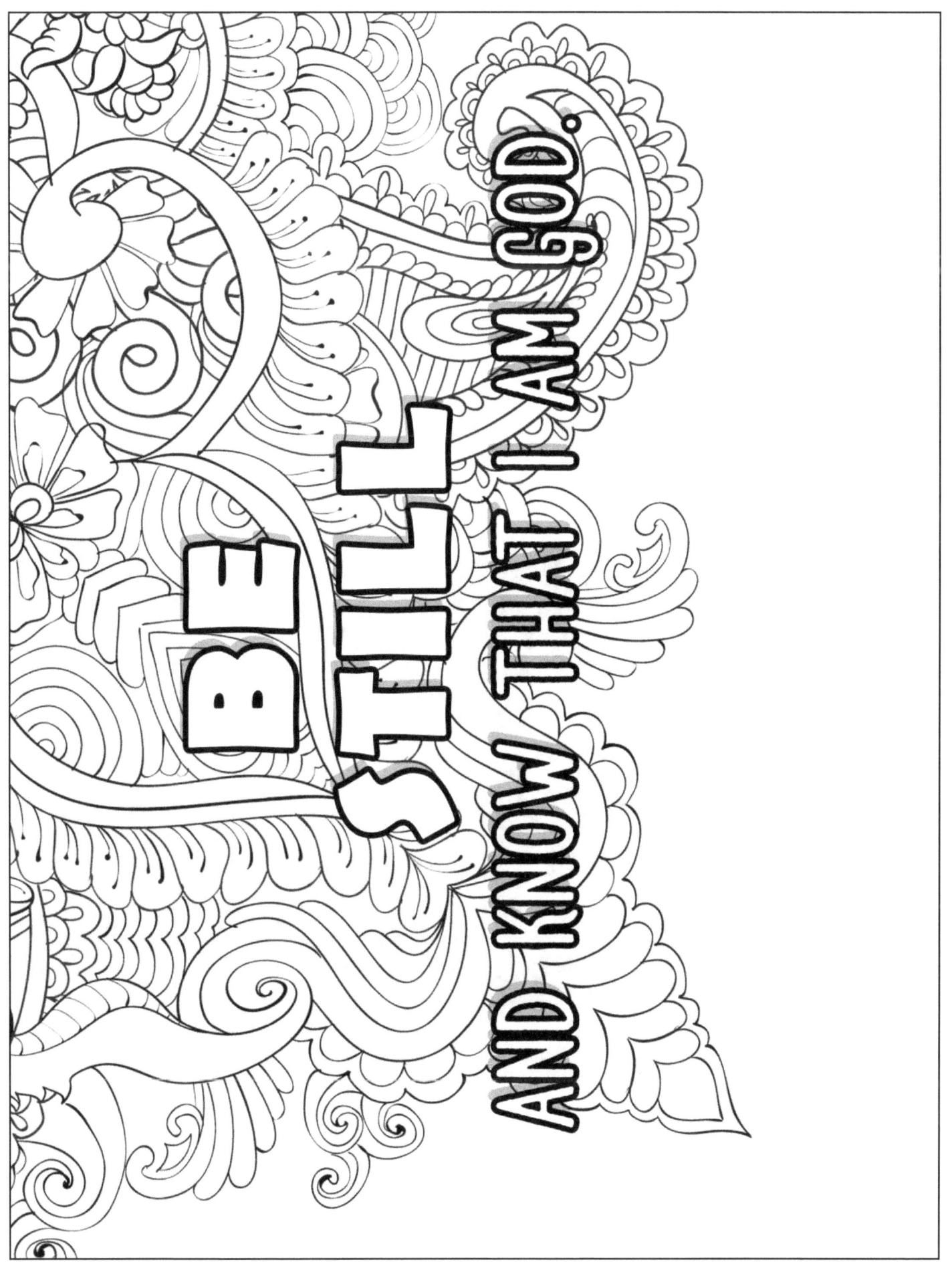

With Quotes From Psalms:

Psalm 4:8
Psalm 16:8
Psalm 23
Psalm 30:6-12
Psalm 34.8
Psalm 42:1, 5
Psalm 51:1-12
Psalm 63
Psalm 84:10-12
Psalm 91
Psalm 139
Psalm 145: 1-16